A Guide to ECR Repository Cleanup

Table of Contents

Chapter 1. Introduction

In this Special Report, we take a deep yet digestible dive into the intricacies of Elastic Container Registry (ECR) Repository Cleanup. As today's world increasingly leans on digital solutions, being savvy with ECR repository management could be the key differentiator in your toolbox. We'll unfold various strategies, techniques, and best practices to maintain a healthy, efficient, and cost-effective ECR environment. Our content, while undeniably technical, is presented in an accessible and down-to-earth language, making it an ideal read for those just wading into this field or seasoned professionals seeking a comprehensive refresh. Through a prudent ECR Repository Cleanup, you can save significant resources and ensure smooth operation; let this report guide you every step of the way.

Chapter 2. Understanding ECR Repository Fundamentals

Amazon Web Services (AWS) provides a fully managed Docker container registry known as Elastic Container Registry (ECR). It makes it simple to store, manage, and deploy Docker container images. ECR's integration with AWS Identity and Access Management (IAM) ensures that repositories are secured. Now that you're aware of ECR, we'll delve deeper to understand its working, and most importantly, the fundamentals of ECR repositories.

2.1. Understanding the Role of Containers

To fully grasp the concept of ECR repositories, we first have to understand what a container is. A container is a standardized unit of software, packaging up the code and its dependencies so that the application runs quickly and reliably from one computing environment to another. A Docker container image is standalone, executable software that includes everything necessary to run a piece of code, including the system tools, system libraries, settings and runtime.

2.2. Docker Images and Containers

Docker images are read-only templates from which Docker containers are launched. These images are created with the build command, and they will produce a container when started with the run command. A Docker image is made up of layers of files stacked on top of each other, with each layer representing an instruction in the image's Dockerfile.

Each layer is only a set of differences from the layer below it. The layers are stacked in such a way that you can see the file system. Docker uses Union file systems (UnionFS) to combine these layers into a single image. UnionFS permits files and directories of separate file systems overlaid, forming a cohesive file system.

2.3. ECR Repositories: A Quick Overview

Now that we've gained an understanding of Docker containers and images, let's explore the concept of ECR repositories. An Amazon ECR repository is a managed location where you can store Docker container images. When you create a repository, you're providing a space where you can push and pull Docker images of your applications. You can create as many repositories as you want and control access to each repository individually.

2.4. The Importance of Structuring ECR Repositories

Proper structuring of ECR repositories is key to maintain the efficiency of a container-focused environment. A well-structured repository enables an efficient retrieval process for container images when needed. This also allows for easy management of image versions which is crucial for rollback, updates, and continuous integration and development.

2.5. Lifecycle Policies in ECR Repositories

As you continually use ECR and implement CI/CD pipelines, older, unutilized Docker images may start to occupy valuable space. Hence, managing your container images becomes crucial. Lifecycle policies in ECR provide an automated solution, ideally configured towards managing image versions within your repositories.

You can define lifecycle rules to manage how images are cleaned up. A lifecycle rule is comprised of a selection - defining what the rule applies to - and an action - outlining what happens when the rule is run. The selection can be based on the tag status (tagged/untagged) and the count type (since image push or image tagged). The action is typically image expiration, often defined with a maximum count or age limit.

2.6. Security Measures in ECR Repositories

AWS ECR provides resource-level controls and IAM policy additions. For instance, when new repositories are created, you can specify the IAM policies for who can access the creations. Through leveraging AWS managed policies, which provide suitable permissions for common use cases, you can govern repository access. Crucially, ECR includes service-linked roles, so it's easy to delegate permissions to AWS services, granting them the ability to perform actions on your resources.

Understanding ECR repository management is critical as it forms the core of your AWS Docker implementation. It impacts your service delivery speed, integrity of your CI/CD pipeline, cost of resources, and the overall security of your cloud environment. Python Boto3, Terraform and AWS CLI are some of the tools you can use to interact with and manage your ECR repositories.

This chapter has walked you through the essential parts of ECR: the role of containers and Docker images in the ECR ecosystem, ECR repositories' structure, formatting, and importance, how to manage image versions through automated lifecycle policies, and security measures in ECR repositories. These are fundamental elements for the successful management of an ECR environment, both in terms of efficiency and cost-effectiveness.

Mastering these fundamentals sets the foundation for more advanced topics, some of which we'll examine in the following chapters such as the actual implementation of ECR repository cleanup processes and how to automate these processes.

Chapter 3. Common Challenges in ECR Repository Maintenance

Keeping an Elastic Container Registry (ECR) tidy and optimized can throw a fair few curveballs your way. The underlying complexities, if not adroitly juggled, can hamper your repository's performance and hike usage costs. So let's delve into some of the most common challenges you may encounter during ECR repository maintenance.

3.1. ECR Image Accumulation Issues

One of the major problems in ECR repository maintenance is unmanaged and unchecked image accumulation. This bloating can significantly increase storage costs on the cloud platform, especially because ECR charges based on the amount of data stored, transferred, and the number of images downloaded.

Developers often overlook the necessity of cleaning up old images, believing that storage space is unlimited. However, this practice can lead to unnecessary clutter, making it arduous to locate specific images among the hundreds or thousands stored. Moreover, these extra images may also hide potential vulnerabilities that jeopardize the entire system.

To mitigate this issue, it's recommendable to implement an automated ECR cleanup process. Automatic removal of nonessential images will ensure that your registry remains lean and manageable. But defining what's 'nonessential' oftentimes becomes a challenge in itself, which we'll confront in the ensuing sections.

3.2. Undefined Retention Policies

A retention policy is critical for maintaining storage efficiency and cost-effectiveness. Many organizations lack defined retention policies for their ECR, leading to accumulation of outdated, erroneous, or simply irrelevant images.

Defining a clear retention policy might require considering several factors. For example, how many versions of a particular image should you keep? How long should an unused image stay in the repository before it gets deleted? These decisions should be based on the nature of your projects and the disk space at your disposal.

Setting up lifecycle policies in ECR can be your bulwarker here. Lifecycle policies enable automatic image pruning based on a specific set of rules, such as the age of an image, the number of image versions to keep, or deleting untagged images.

3.3. Difficulty in Identifying Unused Images

Identifying and removing images no longer in use is essential for optimizing the storage, but this process can be time-consuming and prone to errors. Manual identification of unused images can lead to potential deletion of crucial images, impacting your applications' performance.

Adding complexity, an image deemed 'unused' in a particular environment could be critical in another—illuminating the dire need for synchronized visibility across multiple environments.

A well-built image-usage tracking system can be extremely helpful here, allowing you to track which images are being used across different environments. This system can indicate if an image is indeed dormant or not, helping avoid inadvertent deletion of essential images.

3.4. Handling Vulnerabilities

A major part of ECR repository maintenance involves monitoring for any security vulnerabilities. As stored images might be used across several applications, unmonitored vulnerabilities can leave your entire system exposed to attacks.

The challenge includes identification, prioritization, and rectification of any vulnerabilities found in the images. Amazon ECR provides integrated security vulnerability scans. Nevertheless, setting up regular vulnerability checks, and proactively applying patches or updates is still the best way to manage this concern.

3.5. Maintaining Compliance

Maintaining compliance with industry and local regulations is crucial for any cloud-based service. Be it GDPR, HIPAA, or CCPA - the correct usage and handling of data in your ECR is foundational to conforming to such laws. Noncompliance can result in heavy penalties, not to mention the possible loss of trust from your clients.

The detailed activity log records can assist in demonstrating compliance during audits. However, interpreting these logs and tying them back to specific compliance requirements can be a difficult task.

3.6. Cost Management

As already highlighted, image accumulation in your ECR directly translates into inflated costs. While ECR's pricing is generally straightforward, keeping costs in check requires diligent attention to data transfer and storage practices.

Regularly auditing your ECR, keeping an eye on image usage, and deleting nonessential images will help manage costs. Additionally, employing cost allocation tags can make it easier for you to track your ECR costs on a per-project or per-department basis.

With an understanding of these challenges, you can employ judicious ECR Repository Cleanup strategies to overcome them. As a result, you will not only maintain a healthy ECR environment but also ensure your applications perform optimally while saving costs.

Chapter 4. Introduction to ECR Repository Cleanup

One of the instrumental services offered by Amazon Web Services (AWS) is its registry for Docker images, known as Elastic Container Registry (ECR). ECR allows users to store, manage, and deploy Docker container images. As your application and organization scales, it's natural to accumulate a substantial number of Docker images within your ECR. In due time, as certain images get outdated or unused, it becomes crucial to manage a periodic cleanup to maintain an efficient, cost-effective, and harmonious environment. This introductory chapter seeks to shed light on the umbrella term, 'ECR Repository Cleanup,' its importance, relevance, technical aspects, cleanup procedures, and best practices.

4.1. What is an ECR Repository?

First and foremost, to grasp the meaning and the nuances of ECR Repository Cleanup, it is essential to understand what an ECR Repository is. An ECR Repository is a place where your Docker images are stored. Each Repository can contain multiple versions of an image, and you can use it to push and pull different versions of the same Docker image. Therefore, as far as storage in the realm of Amazon ECR is considered, ECR Repositories are the linchpin.

4.2. Why ECR Repository Cleanup?

A rigorous strategy for ECR Repository Cleanup comes with a plethora of benefits. Here are a few:

1. Cost-Efficiency: As each image stored in the ECR Repository incurs a cost, eliminating unnecessary, outdated Docker images could lead to significant monetary savings.

2. Operational Efficiency: Removing superfluous images from your repository makes its management more manageable, leading to a more seamless operation.

3. Avoiding Repository Overcrowding: Overcrowding can lead to additional burdens such as difficulty in finding necessary images swiftly. Hence, cleanup ensures easy management and usability.

4. Security Considerations: Outdated or unused images might have vulnerabilities. Cleaning these up helps maintain a securer environment.

Therefore, we cannot overstate the importance of ECR Repository Cleanup.

4.3. Understanding Docker Images Life-cycle

Recognizing the different stages of the Docker Images life-cycle is a prerequisite for effective ECR Repository Cleanup. The life-cycle can be summarized as follows:

1. Create: Development teams create Docker images and push them to the ECR Repository.

2. Use: These Docker images are pulled and used in various environments.

3. Deprecate: As time passes, these Docker images may become outdated or unused.

4. Identify: The outdated, unused Docker images are identified for removal.

5. Clean: The identified Docker Images are deleted from the ECR Repository.

The identification and cleaning of Docker Images form the crux of the ECR Repository Cleanup

4.4. ECR Repository Cleanup Strategies

An appropriate cleanup strategy is tailored according to the organization's specific requirements. It usually involves understanding the Docker Image usage pattern, defining what constitutes an 'Unused Docker Image,' choosing the right tools and automation techniques, and a continuous monitoring system.

4.5. ECR Repository Cleanup Techniques

There are multiple methods to achieve ECR Repository Cleanup. The chosen technique depends on factors like the number of images, the usage pattern, and the acceptable risk levels for the organization. Some popular techniques include manual removal, script-based removal, using AWS Management Console, and AWS CLI or SDKs.

4.6. Best Practices for ECR Repository Cleanup

Follow these best practices for a productive, systematic, and efficient cleanup procedure:

1. Regularly Audit your ECR Repository: This helps detect outdated, infrequently used Docker images.

2. Implement Automated Cleanup: Setup automated solutions to regularly clean up unnecessary Docker images. Tools like Lifecycle Policies can be very helpful.

3. Define Clear Policies: Establish and communicate clear policies on the retention and discarding of Docker images.

4. Test Before Full Execution: Before employing a new cleanup technique or tool, run it on a small scale to analyse the results.

5. Regular Reviews: Regular reviews of the cleanup strategy and execution are necessary to ensure efficacy and improving it over time.

In summary, ECR Repository Cleanup is a vital task in maintaining a cost-effective and smooth-running ECR environment. With a clear understanding of the Docker images life-cycle and employing appropriate strategies, techniques, and best practices, a systematic cleanup can be achieved. In the ensuing chapters, we will delve deeper into the technical aspects and detailed walkthroughs of various cleanup techniques.

Chapter 5. Effective Strategies for Deleting Old Docker Images

Dealing with old Docker images in your ECR repository presents a unique challenge: how do you strike the right balance between maintaining access to older builds for potential rollbacks, and the need to control costs, as well as avoid cluttering your environment with outdated and possibly insecure resources? Here, we'll address a range of effective strategies specifically designed for the efficient deletion of old Docker images.

5.1. Start with a Strategy

The first step towards maintaining a clean, efficient ECR repository involves establishing a concrete strategy. Whether you prefer manual deletion, lifecycle policies, or third-party cleaning tools, having a clear plan in place will help streamline the task of repository cleanup. Start by assessing your current repository status, then decide which images can be removed, which need to be retained, and how often this process should be repeated.

5.2. Manual Pruning

Basic Docker offers a few commands to manually prune old, unused, or dangling images, such as `docker image prune` or `docker rmi $(docker images -q)`. However, performing such commands on a regular basis can become time-consuming, particularly in larger organizations where massive amounts of images are continuously being created.

5.3. Lifecycle Policies: An Automated Solution

Amazon ECR Lifecycle Policies provide an automatic, policy-based approach to managing the lifecycle of images in your repositories. To create a Lifecycle Policy, navigate to your ECR repository in the AWS Management Console, select the repository and click on "Lifecycle Policies." Here, you can create rules that specify when to remove old Docker images based on various conditions, like image age or tag status.

The Lifecycle Policy rule syntax is declarative – it states what outcome you want and lets AWS determine how to achieve it. For example:

```
{
  "rules": [
    {
      "rulePriority": 1,
      "description": "Remove untagged images",
      "selection": {
        "tagStatus": "untagged",
        "countType": "imageCountMoreThan",
        "countNumber": 100
      },
      "action": {
        "type": "expire"
      }
    }
  ]
}
```

This policy will keep only the last 100 untagged images per repository and remove all previous (older) ones. You can create similar rules for tagged images or add more complex conditions. Remember that rules are processed in order of priority, with lower numbers getting processed first.

5.4. Leverage CLI

CLI (Command Line Interface) is another handy, albeit technical, approach to prune old Docker images. AWS CLI provides commands for interacting with ECR and, combined with shell scripting, can afford granular control over image deletion.

With CLI, you can filter images based on tags, creation date, or other parameters. For instance, execute the `list-images` command to retrieve a list of images in a repository, then loop through and remove the outdated ones.

However, keep in mind that CLI is an advanced tool. Make sure to thoroughly test any scripts in a safe environment before deploying them in a production setting to avoid accidental data loss.

5.5. Third-Party Tools: Docker Prune and Others

Outside Docker, there are other dedicated tools for pruning old images, such as Docker Prune, Docker GC (Garbage Collector), and commercial tools like Quay.io by Red Hat. These tools offer robust clean-up operations which can be scheduled and customized according to your requirements.

Docker Prune is a native Docker command that removes all unused images. Docker GC, on the other hand, is an open-source script for cleaning up Docker hosts. As a commercial solution, Quay.io offers automated image cleanup as part of their service, should you opt for their platform.

Despite their evident convenience, it's important to approach third-party tools with caution - not all tools might suit your environment, and each comes with its own pros and cons. Therefore, it is crucial to evaluate these options thoroughly before selection.

5.6. Keep Security in Mind

One crucial aspect to remember during Docker image cleanup is to ensure older images that might contain vulnerabilities are not left unattended. Running regular vulnerability scans on your ECR repositories using tools like AWS ECR Image Scanning or open-source alternatives like Clair, can help identify and remove such images. By incorporating this practice into your routine, you can maintain a healthier, more secure image repository.

In conclusion, there's no one-size-fits-all solution to deleting old Docker images; it's a process that needs to be tailored to fit individual organizational needs and practices. Regardless of the chosen method, it should become a regular part of your ECR repository management to ensure efficiency, cost-effectiveness, and a clean working environment. With a well-planned strategy and careful consideration of the tools and techniques available, organizations can maintain an optimal ECR environment.

Chapter 6. The Role of Lifecycle Policies in ECR Cleanup

To kickstart our exploration, it's crucial we first unpack the role of lifecycle policies in ECR Cleanup, the bedrock of efficient repository management.

Undeniably, lifecycle policies operate as the heart that pumps efficiency into the system. These policies provide a framework for managing your images, including defining when images are outdated and when they should be automatically deleted to free up storage space.

6.1. Understanding Lifecycle Policies

A lifecycle policy, in its simplest form, is a set of rules. These rules guide the preservation or removal of Docker images based on criteria such as the age of an image, the time of the last pull, or even a specific tag. If you're wondering how this matters to ECR Cleanup, the rationale is straightforward. With a well-structured lifecycle policy, you keep your repository free from unnecessary resource consumption while retaining images pertinent to your operations, thereby reducing costs and enhancing efficiency.

6.2. Crafting Your Lifecycle Policy

A solid lifecycle policy begins with addressing a few pivotal questions: - Which images should stay preserved within the repository, and for how long? - Which images should be pruned, and what's the respective timeline? - What are the image expiry factors to consider?

Aligning Lifecycle Policy with Business Needs

```
    Prioritizing images you frequently use or with tags
indicating production environment ensures your system
runs uninterrupted, while less important images can be
set to auto-expire after a specified timeframe.
```

Take a reflective look at your operations and identify the answers to these questions. That's your first step in creating a lifecycle policy that both fits your requirements and optimizes your ECR repository.

6.3. Implementing Lifecycle Policies

Once a policy has been established, it's time for implementation. This is done through the 'PutLifecyclePolicy' AWS CLI command or the AWS Management Console. Provide your policy as a JSON file and specify image selection criteria and action for the policy.

Example JSON file for Lifecycle policy

```
{
  "rules": [
    {
      "rulePriority": 1,
      "description": "Expire images older than 14 days",
      "selection": {
        "tagStatus": "untagged",
        "countType": "sinceImagePushed",
        "countUnit": "days",
        "countNumber": 14
      },
      "action": {
```

```
        "type": "expire"
      }
    }
  ]
}
```

The illustration above depicts a simple policy that specifies the expiration of untagged images 14 days after they're pushed.

6.4. Lifecycle Policy Rules

Within a lifecycle policy, you can create rules to shape the treatment of your Docker images. Consider this; you have an image tagged `production` that is necessary for your operations. You wouldn't want this image to be auto-deleted after a day or two. A rule within your lifecycle policy ensures this image isn't pruned.

Multiple rules can be defined within a single policy; however, each must bear a unique `rulePriority` number. The lower the number, the higher the priority of the rule, and this comes into play when an image meets the criteria of multiple rules.

6.5. Optimizing Lifecycle Policies Over Time

A good lifecycle policy isn't a set-it-and-forget-it solution; it evolves with your business. As your needs change, so should the parameters of your policy. An annual review of your policy helps in identifying any required adjustments. As your service scales, the repository's images may increase drastically - thus, policy rules should be optimized to support this growth while maintaining the repository's efficiency.

In conclusion, understanding the role of lifecycle policies as the silent architects of an efficient ECR environment is fundamental. Whether you're defining, implementing, or adjusting these policies, each phase plays a decisive part in managing your ECR repository, making ECR Cleanup a breeze. As you forge ahead, remember the aim: an optimized ecosystem that marries cost-effectiveness with operational efficiency. Furthermore, the happy balance offsets your data usage while ensuring your business-critical services remain uninterrupted.

Chapter 7. Automating the ECR Repository Cleanup Process

Before we delve deeper into automating the ECR Repository Cleanup process, it's important to familiarize ourselves with why automation is crucial. Automation not only frees up time for developers to concentrate on feature development but also prevents manual mistakes, making the cleanup process consistent and reliable. Moreover, it fosters timeliness and periodic checks, ensuring optimal resource management.

7.1. The Importance of Automation

Automation has emerged as an essential ingredient in modern software development practices. With the repeated pattern of deployments in the DevOps world, manually managing resources like ECR repositories is not only time-consuming but also unnecessary when we have the technology to automate these tasks effectively.

Manually cleaning up ECR repositories can be error-prone and inconsistent, and it may not even be feasible for larger systems with more repositories. As a result, automating this process not only reduces human intervention but also ensures a more reliable and consistent cleanup.

To illustrate the effectiveness of automation, consider a situation where a development team deploys multiple services daily, each deployment pushing a new Docker image to ECR. With dozens or possibly hundreds of images created every week, managing these resources becomes a cumbersome task and poses risk of using more storage than needed, thus escalating costs. Automating the ECR Repository Cleanup process helps efficiently tackle this issue.

7.2. Automating using Lifecycle Policies

One approach to automate this cleanup process is by leveraging lifecycle policies provided by AWS. By implementing these policies, you can define rules to clean up your repositories at regular intervals.

Lifecycle policies are rule-based, where you can specify a set of match criteria and an action to perform when those match criteria are met. For ECR, these policies clean up unused Docker images.

How it works:

1. Create a Lifecycle Policy JSON

This JSON document is where you specify the rules to manage your images. Each rule consists of 'rulePriority', 'description', 'selection' and 'action'.

1. Attach the policy to ECR repository

Once your policy is ready, you can attach it to a particular ECR repository or multiple repositories.

1. Monitor the Cleanup

AWS provides mechanisms to monitor the lifecycle policy executions. These mechanisms allow you to stay informed about what images are being deleted and when, helping you make necessary adjustments to your policies if needed.

7.3. AWS CLI for ECR Cleanup

If you want to extend beyond the lifecycle policies and need more flexibility and granular control, AWS CLI (AWS Command Line

Interface) can be a powerful tool. With AWS CLI, you can create a cleanup script that can be tailor-made to suit specific needs. For instance, you can choose to preserve the latest N images or delete images older than N days, and these controls are not limited to a repository but can span across multiple repositories, or within a given namespace.

The script would majorly consist of two commands:

1. List Images

Use 'aws ecr list-images' command to get a list of your Docker images.

1. Batch Delete-Image

'aws ecr batch-delete-image' command can then be used to delete the unneeded images.

This script can be scheduled to run periodically according to your cleanup strategy, thus automating the cleanup process.

7.4. Using AWS Lambda for Cleanup

AWS Lambda is another powerful service that can be employed to automate ECR cleanup. With Lambda, you can run your code without provisioning or managing servers, offering a straightforward way to run your cleanup script.

Your code can be triggered by various AWS services or can be scheduled to run at regular intervals. In the context of ECR cleanup, you can trigger your Lambda function based on events such as repository creation, or schedule it to run daily, weekly etc.

The Lambda function would consist of two steps similar to the CLI approach: List Images and Batch Delete-Image. However, in addition to this, it provides capabilities for logging, error handling, and scalability that can enhance the automation process.

7.5. Conclusion: The best approach

Choosing the best approach to automate your ECR Repository Cleanup process depends on various factors such as your system size, the diversity in your repositories, your specific needs and constraints. One thing is clear, though: Automation is critical for managing your ECR environment efficiently. By choosing the right automation strategy, you'll save valuable time, reduce costs, and prevent potential discrepancies caused by manual interventions. This commitment to cleanliness, efficiency, and smart utilization of cloud resources will ultimately serve to improve and streamline your software development practices.

Chapter 8. Securing Your ECR Repository During Cleanup

Security for your Amazon ECR repositories should always be a top concern. Proper security measures ensure that your image data is not corrupted, lost, or accessed without authorization. When embarking on a clean-up operation, there are various strategies to secure repositories and their contents.

8.1. Implementing Access Control

Access controls are a great starting line for your ECR repository security strategy. AWS employs Identity and Access Management (IAM) policies to provide secure and fine-grained access control to your ECR repositories.

To implement access control:

1. Navigate to the IAM console in your AWS account.

2. Create an IAM policy that includes the necessary rights to access the ECR repository.

3. Attach the policy to an IAM user, group, or role.

4. Confirm that the user, group, or role can pull and push images from the repository, but only as authorized in the IAM policy.

This intentional, role-based control prevents unauthorized access and modifications to the repository, facilitating secure cleanup operations.

8.2. Lifecycle Policy

A lifecycle policy can be an effective tool for automating the cleanup process of your repositories. Lifecycles define rules to manage your images, such as automatically deleting underutilized or outdated images.

However, in developing lifecycle policies for your repositories, consider factoring in exceptions. These can protect necessary images from inadvertent deletion during the cleanup; thus, effectively serving as a security measure. Here's a simple example of a lifecycle policy:

```
{
  "rules": [
    {
      "rulePriority": 1,
      "description": "Clear images older than 30 days",
      "selection": {
        "tagStatus": "untagged",
        "countType": "sinceImagePushed",
        "countUnit": "days",
        "countNumber": 30
      },
      "action": { "type": "expire" }
    }
  ]
}
```

This lifecycle policy removes all untagged images that were pushed to the ECR repository more than 30 days ago. The "rulePriority" field defines the order in which rules are evaluated. Lower numbers denote higher priority.

8.3. Audit Trail

Another critical point is to establish an audit trail for the cleanup process. AWS CloudTrail is a resource that allows tracking user activity and API usage, thereby providing a history of changes made to the ECR repository, which can be crucial during investigations if anything goes wrong.

Consider integrating AWS CloudTrail with Amazon CloudWatch for real-time monitoring and to set alerts for abnormalities. It helps you spot any unexpected user action on the repository during and after the cleanup operation.

8.4. Securing Network Access

Securing network access protects your repositories from threats at the network level. Be sure to follow best practices, such as:

1. Enable AWS PrivateLink to prevent data transmission over the public Internet.

2. Constrain inbound and outbound traffic using Security Group rules.

3. Implement network Access Control Lists (ACLs) to deny unknown IP addresses access to your repositories.

Provisioning secure network access minimizes the risk of cyber threats during cleanup.

8.5. Image Scanning

Last but not least, use the built-in image scanning feature of ECR regularly. This analyzes the Docker images for any known vulnerabilities. It's a valuable security measure to run before and after any cleanup operation. A clean bill of health for your images guarantees the security of the ECR environment post-cleanup.

In conclusion, securing your ECR repository during cleanup isn't just about removing old or unnecessary images; it's about maintaining a secure environment before, during, and after any operation. Remember, when fully optimized, a secured and cleaned ECR repository results in a safer, more cost-effective, and highly efficient storage system. The tools provided by AWS, including IAM, Lifecycle Policies, CloudTrail, PrivateLink, and ECR image scanning, provide a robust set of tools to secure your cleanup process.

Chapter 9. Case Study: Successful ECR Repository Cleanup

The organization at the heart of our case study is a mid-sized tech firm - let's call them TechFirm for confidentiality's sake. TechFirm relies heavily on AWS services and equally heavily on Docker/container-based deployments in their day-to-day operations. They ran into an issue when they reached the ECR repository limit. They noticed this issue while trying to push new Docker images to ECR. From this point, they decided to embark on an ECR Repository cleanup journey.

9.1. The Initial Issue

When TechFirm realized they reached the aforementioned ECR repository limit, they initially tried to delete a few Docker images manually. This approach, while potentially viable for smaller organizations, quickly proved inefficient and untenable. Docker images are often split into hundreds, if not thousands, of parts, each being its own distinct image. Manually tracking and removing these images bogs down the process and opens the door for human error.

9.2. Embracing Automation

Recognizing the inefficiency of manual cleanup, TechFirm decided to adopt an automated cleanup strategy. They wrote scripts using AWS Command-Line Interface (CLI) to identify and delete older, underused Docker images.

```
#!/bin/bash
```

```bash
# This script is designed to clean up repository by
deleting older images

REPO_NAME='your_repo_name'
PROFILE_NAME='aws_profile_name'

aws ecr list-images --repository-name $REPO_NAME
--profile $PROFILE_NAME --query
'imageIds[*].[imageDigest]' --output text | while read
-r line ; do
aws ecr batch-delete-image --repository-name $REPO_NAME
--profile $PROFILE_NAME --image-ids imageDigest=$line
done
```

The success of this script depends on predefining certain details, like the repository name and AWS profile name. However, it's important to remember that this script would indiscriminately delete all images in the repository, irrespective of their viable usage or age.

9.3. Implementing Intelligent Cleanup

TechFirm quickly realized the need to refine their cleanup strategy. Deleting all images was not sustainable or practical. There was a high risk of erasing recent, meaningful Docker images.

To address this, they, further refined their scripting efforts to intelligently identify and delete Docker images. Now, their script, rather than indiscriminately pruning everything, only removed Docker images that were older than a specified number of days (30 days in their case). This ensured that any recent or frequently used data would be preserved while cutting out the redundant clutter.

```bash
#!/bin/bash
```

```bash
# This script cleans up repository by deleting older
images, preserving recent ones

REPO_NAME='your_repo_name'
PROFILE_NAME='aws_profile_name'
DAYS=30


CURRENT_TIME=$(date +%s)
DELETE_TIME=$((CURRENT_TIME - (DAYS * 86400)))


aws ecr list-images --repository-name $REPO_NAME
--profile $PROFILE_NAME --query
'imageIds[*].[imageDigest]' --output text | while read
-r line ; do
IMAGE_PUSHED_TIME=`aws ecr describe-images --repository
-name $REPO_NAME --profile $PROFILE_NAME --image-ids
imageDigest=$line --query
'imageDetails[*].[imagePushedAt]' --output text`


if [[ $IMAGE_PUSHED_TIME -le $DELETE_TIME  ]]; then
aws ecr batch-delete-image --repository-name $REPO_NAME
--profile $PROFILE_NAME --image-ids imageDigest=$line
fi
done
```

9.4. Streamlining With Lifecycle Policy

Though the second script significantly improved on their initial approach, TechFirm realized that using CLI scripts still required regular, manual invocations. Plus, it lacked the subtlety of finer-grained selection criteria that ECR lifecycle policies could offer.

Upon exploring ECR lifecycle policies, they discovered that these policies provided precise rules for ECR to automatically clean up Docker images. Lifecycle policies indeed proved to be the efficient, expressive and cost-effective solution that TechFirm sought from the start.

```
{
  "rules": [
    {
      "rulePriority": 1,
      "description": "Expire images older than 30 days",
      "selection": {
        "tagStatus": "untagged",
        "countType": "sinceImagePushed",
        "countUnit": "days",
        "countNumber": 30
      },
      "action": {
        "type": "expire"
      }
    }
  ]
}
```

This lifecycle policy setup enabled TechFirm to delete any untagged Docker images that were older than 30 days, leading to a smoother repository management overall.

9.5. Evaluating Outcomes and Achievements

In the end, TechFirm saw a dramatic improvement in their ECR repository management. By employing AWS CLI scripts and ECR lifecycle policies, they effectively automated the cumbersome cleanup process, saving both time and resources. Moreover, this intelligent cleanup approach allowed TechFirm to keep useful Docker images at their disposal.

The reduction in storage space directly converted into cost-savings while boosting team productivity due to the speedy retrieval of valuable images. The time and efforts saved let TechFirm's developers focus on their main tasks, turning this cleanup initiative into a structural win for the company.

By sharing TechFirm's journey towards an effective ECR Repository Cleanup, we hope to guide you on an equally successful path. Heeding the struggles and successes of TechFirm, you can exploit the potential of a well-managed ECR environment and cement your place in your field.

Chapter 10. Cost Analysis: Regular ECR Cleanup vs Neglected Repository

Understanding the economic implications of regular ECR cleanup versus a neglected repository requires us to address a combination of direct and indirect costs associated with each approach. Consequently, this analysis unfolds from the perspective of storage and data transfer costs, operational efficiency, potential downtime, and the overall impact on the customer and team productivity.

10.1. Direct Costs: Storage and Data Transfer

The most immediate cost incurred with ECR repositories is the storage and data transfer cost. AWS ECR pricing is primarily storage-based, with charges per GB-month consumed. However, costs can also accrue from data transfer operations, especially when executed across different regions.

Regular cleanup of old and unutilized images helps maintain a lighter repository, thereby, minimizing the storage cost. In contrast, a repository left unchecked will accumulate every new image pushed into it, which can inflate the storage costs over time. Besides, such swollen repositories may necessitate considerable data transfer operations, bearing additional costs due to cross-region data movements.

Moreover, the cost implications can further escalate in scenarios where dev teams make frequent pushes into the ECR repository. Undeniably, these activities increase the storage footprint but removing unneeded and old images on a regular cadence justifies the costs.

Let's visualize this with a hypothetical example:

Image Creation Rate	Cleanup Strategy	Average Images/month	Total Storage/month (GB)	Estimated Cost/month (USD)
10/day	Regular	300	150	3.75
10/day	Neglected	900	450	11.25

As clearly exemplified, regular cleanup offers significant savings over a neglected repository, and these savings can quickly accumulate over time.

10.2. Indirect Costs: Operational Efficiency and Downtime

Storage and data transfer costs only scratch the surface of the potential economic cost of an neglected ECR repository. Operational efficiency, or lack thereof, can prove even more costly. Layers of unused and outdated images can slow down your cash burn at a rate faster than AWS can bill you for it.

In a cluttered repository, finding relevant images, parsing through versions, and even pushing new images can become a tedious process. This chain reaction can take away valuable time from your development cycle, leading to missed deadlines, slower product upgrades, and lost opportunities. Ultimately, the cost of these inefficiencies are borne by the organization as they reduce the team's capacity to deliver value.

Similarly, neglecting ECR cleanup can increase the risk of downtime, another significant cost center. As repositories grow bloated and unwieldy, they become more susceptible to failures, which can lead to service outages. Downtime carries with it not just the cost of lost productivity, but potentially also customer churn due to poor user experience.

10.3. ROI - Calculating the Payoff

Whereas neglecting ECR cleanup can lead to escalating short and long term costs, investing in regular repository cleanups has its costs too. There's the time spent planning and implementing the cleanup strategy, potential operational hiccups, and possibly some up-front costs if automation tools are brought into play.

However, when these inputs are stacked against the potential savings from avoided storage, data transfer costs, improved operational efficiency and reduced downtime, the return on investment can be quite appealing. Regardless of the size of your team, computational requirement, or the rate of image pushes, a well-executed cleanup strategy can liberate resources, monetary or otherwise, for more value-driven operations.

Adjusting the lens from absolute numbers to productivity and long-term customer value highlights the benefits of regular repository cleanup more distinctly. A smoother operation infuses confidence in your development cycle, helping maintain, if not broaden, your market footprint over time.

In conclusion, regular ECR repository cleanup, albeit seemingly simple and mundane, plays a crucial role in resource optimization and operational excellence. A neglected repository may not appear threatening in the short-term, but in the long run, it can silently drain a company's resources while hampering the nimbleness of your development team. Act proactively, consider the overall costs, and leverage the savings potential to your benefit.

Chapter 11. Preparing for the Future: Scalable ECR Cleanup Strategies

Sandwiched between the immediate necessities of tidying up your Elastic Container Registry (ECR) and the potential gravity of ignoring it, lies the art and science of scalable cleanup strategies - the future-proofing of your container artifacts' housekeeping.

This approach entails keen foresight, strategic planning, effective execution, coupled with continuous monitoring and adjustment. It ensures not just an organized and efficient repository today, but more importantly, one that can cope with the scale, complexity, and diversity of your growing business demands tomorrow.

11.1. Embracing Automation

As your ECR environment becomes increasingly robust, manually cleaning up repositories isn't just impractical; it might be virtually impossible. Consider automation as your ally – one that will take over repetitive, mundane tasks, freeing you and your team to focus on mission-critical projects.

Among the popular automation services to consider is AWS Lambda. By creating a function to regularly sweep through your repositories, old or unused images can be removed. AWS provides sample scripts that can be adjusted to suit your needs. The script can be set to trigger at regular intervals or based on specific events using CloudWatch Events.

Shell scripts are another option to automate your cleanup processes. Running a script as a cron job on a daily, weekly, or monthly basis will help you maintain a lean repository.

11.2. Infrastructure as Code (IAC)

IAC is a solid foundation in building scalable solutions. With regards to ECR, it allows you to manage repositories much like application code, enabling efficient versioning, team collaboration, and more importantly, effective cleanup strategies.

AWS's CloudFormation simplifies IAC adoption. Defining your resources in YAML or JSON templates would make it easier for you to spin up or tear down environments as necessary, and as fast as your text editor can save the file.

Terraform by HashiCorp is another powerful IAC tool. While CloudFormation is AWS-centric, Terraform is provider-agnostic. Familiarize yourself with Terraform if your ECR is cohabitating with resources outside AWS.

Leveraging IAC also means your cleanup process can be scripted and versioned, thus making it reusable and scalable.

11.3. Lifecycle Policies

Perhaps one of the most important cleanup tools at your disposal is ECR's Lifecycle Policies. This versatile feature allows you to define rules for your image cleanup, based on factors like image type, tag status, and age. These rules can run either manually or automatically.

Lifecycle Policies bring significant benefits:

- It ensures a regular clean-up of old or unused images.

- It helps in reducing storage costs.

- It simplifies the management of your repositories.

Remember, managing ECR lifecycle policies as part of your IAC strategy enhances their power, as they can be.version-controlled and easily replicated across different repositories.

11.4. Team Training & Culture

Lastly, the human factor cannot be overemphasized. Automation and policies will do much of the heavy lifting, but they need to be set up and monitored by skilled human beings.

Your team needs continuous training about the importance of cleanup, how to create Lifecycle Policies, how to write automation scripts, and the power of IAC. Keep everyone up to speed on the latest tools and industry strategies. Encourage questions and provide assistance. Remember, your cleanup strategy is as strong as the weakest link in your team.

A culture that values cleanliness in data and process management is the very core of an effective and scalable ECR cleanup strategy. This involves cultivating a wider sense of responsibility for both creating and cleaning-up container images.

In conclusion, preparing for the future entails more than just staying on top of day-to-day cleanup tasks, it demands strategically directed actions toward a well-maintained, scalable, and future-proof ECR environment. By adopting the right toolset, automation, lifecycle management, and cultivating an informed, conscientious team, your ECR cleanup strategy will lead to efficient and cost-effective operations for the long run.